An Amazing Catch

AMERICAN BIBLE SOCIETY
NEW YORK

An Amazing Catch (Vol. 10)
Scripture quotes from the *Contemporary English Version,* Luke 5.1-11 (CEV).
Wording and grammar represent the kind of language best understood
and appreciated by young readers.

Copyright © 1995, American Bible Society
1865 Broadway, New York, N. Y. 10023
www.americanbible.org

Illustrations by Chantal Muller van den Berghe
Text by Bernard Hubler and Claude-Bernard Costecalde, Ph. D.
Design by Jacques Rey

Copyright © 1997, Éditions du Signe
Strasbourg, France

ISBN 1-58516-175-6
Printed in Italy
Eng. Port. CEV 560 P - 109867
ABS - 7/00 - 5,000

4

Jesus prepared his closest friends to be in charge of the community that he was going to set up.

To show them what this was all about, he taught them and he gave them some signs, called "miracles." Once, he cured a blind man; another time he fed a huge crowd of people using just a few loaves and fishes.

Today we find him in a boat with his friends.

Such an amazing thing happens that they decide to leave everything and follow him.

5

Then Jesus sat down in the boat
to teach the crowd.

Jesus loved talking to the crowd.
They gathered all around him.
So that everyone could hear him,
he got into Simon's boat
and asked him to pull away
from the shore.
Everyone listened to him carefully.

If you have something important to say,
there's always someone who will listen.

He told Simon, "Row the boat out into deeper water and let your nets down."

Jesus had finished teaching the crowd.
He said to Simon: "Go out into deeper water
and then, if you cast your nets,
you'll catch some fish."
Simon seemed surprised.
He didn't budge.
He frowned and shook his head.

*There are lots of words which surprise us,
but we have to find out what they mean.*

Simon answered, "We have worked hard all night long and have not caught a thing."

Simon was good at his job as a fisherman. He said to Jesus: "We've been fishing all night without catching anything. It's not a good time for fishing; there won't be any fish today."

It's hard to accept that you're wrong.

"But if you tell me to, I will let the nets down."

When Jesus insisted,
Simon sighed and said,
   "Right, since you say so, I'll cast out the nets."
He shouted to his work-mates,
      "Come on guys! Let's get on with it
      and cast out the nets!"

*When you trust someone,
you do what he or she asks.*

They did it and caught so many fish that their nets began ripping apart.

A strange thing happened.
   The fishermen could hardly lift their nets
      back on board. They were so full
         that they were almost bursting.
            "What great fish!" said some of them.
            "Careful! The net's tearing," cried others.

Trusting another person leads to new experiences.

They signaled for their partners in the other boat to come and help them.

Not far from there, some of their friends were watching the whole thing from another boat.

"Quick! Come and help us!" shouted Simon.

"OK, we're coming!" they shouted back to him. And they began to row with all their might.

We don't keep good things to ourselves; we share them with others.

Together they filled the two boats.

What wonderful fish!
The men leaned over
and hauled in the nets.
The two boats, full to overflowing,
almost began to sink.

Patience and effort are always rewarded.

When Simon Peter saw this happen, he knelt down in front of Jesus and said, "Lord, don't come near me!"

Simon, who was also called Peter,
knew that Jesus was an exceptional person.

He threw himself at Jesus' feet and said,
"Don't come near me Lord,
for I'm just a poor sinner."
He and his friends
trembled with fear.

*You learn to get to know a person better
if you go through something difficult with them.*

Jesus told Simon, "Don't be afraid! From now on you will bring in people instead of fish."

Jesus comforted him and said,
"Don't be frightened, my friend,
from now on it's people
that you will be catching!"
Jesus was thinking of all those people
that Simon Peter would later gather
into the great family of Jesus' friends.
This family is called the Church.

Because God loves all men and women, he wants to gather them into the net of his love.

The men pulled their boats up on the shore. Then they left everything and went with Jesus.

What happened to the fish?
No one will ever know!
What happened to Simon Peter and his friends?
They became disciples of Jesus.
That means they were
his faithful friends who left everything
to follow him, always and everywhere.

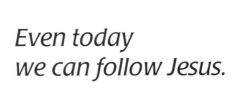

*Even today
we can follow Jesus.*

What an amazing catch!
However, what really counts
isn't the huge number of fish,
but Jesus' words to Simon Peter:
"It's people you will be catching."
Jesus was going to set up a community, the Church.
And his friends would be in charge of it.
Simon Peter and his friends
wouldn't catch people to throw them in prison.
That would be like a horrible net of fear.
Instead, they would gather people into the net of love,
because God loves all the men and women of the world.

Then Jesus sat down in the boat to teach the crowd.

He told Simon, "Row the boat out into deeper water and let your nets down."

Simon answered, "We have worked hard all night long and have not caught a thing."

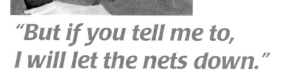

"But if you tell me to, I will let the nets down."

They did it and caught so many fish that their nets began ripping apart.

They signaled for their partners in the other boat to come and help them.

Together they filled the two boats.

When Simon Peter saw this happen, he knelt down in front of Jesus and said, "Lord, don't come near me!"

Jesus told Simon, "Don't be afraid! From now on you will bring in people instead of fish."

The men pulled their boats up on the shore. Then they left everything and went with Jesus.

IN THE SAME COLLECTIONS:

The Good Samaritan
The Paralyzed Man
Zacchaeus
On the Road to Emmaus
Bartimaeus
The Call of the Disciples
The Calming of the Storm
Shared Bread
The Prodigal Son
The Forgiven Sinner
The Farmer Who Went Out To Sow